Our Story Book

PHOTO ALBUM & SCRAPBOOK FOR COUPLES

This amazing book belongs to the beautiful couple:

....

&

....

How can you use this Book?

Our Adventure Book is the perfect keepsake gift for couples. It is made with High-quality paper and designed with love that will accurately keep your memories about a special day. Below are 100 conversation starter questions that you can use to write your thoughts.

On the left side, you can glue a photo, draw something silly or just write down the conversation starter that you picked up to discuss with your partner. You can use this book anywhere: when you are traveling, camping, at your best friend's wedding, in holidays...etc. On the right side, you can write a small description of what happened that day, or you can write down your opinions on the conversation starter that you picked.

This beautiful scrapbook is designed for couples and it's meant to be used on any occasion. It is the perfect anniversary gift, valentines day gift or it can be used as a present for any other special moment you cherish.

Deep Conversation Starters about your Relationship:

1. If you could change one thing about our relationship, what would it be?
2. What can I do to be a better partner?
3. What do you think is the most annoying thing about me?
4. Do you think we have good communication in our relationship, or do you think we can improve?
5. What do you like best about me?
6. What do you like the least about me?
7. Do you believe in "soulmates" and, if so, do you think that I am your soulmate?
8. Are you content with our relationship, as is?
9. What do you think your life would be like without me?
10. What do you think is the key to a successful relationship?
11. Which do you value more in a relationship, comfort or spontaneity?
12. What do you think a woman's role should be in a relationship?

13. What do you think a man's role should be in a relationship?
14. What are 3 things that I can do to make you feel more appreciated?
15. Do you think we spend too much time together, or not enough?
16. What is one thing you wish I did differently as a parent?
17. Do you think that I've made you a better person, and if so, how?
18. What has been your favorite memory of our time together?
19. What is one thing you would change about our sex life?
20. What was the moment that you first knew you loved me?
21. What is one thing that can help me know YOU better?
22. What do think is your greatest strength in our relationship?
23. Is there something that I do that makes you feel disrespected?
24. Why do you think I am "the One"?
25. Do I have all of the traits that you look for in a partner?
26. When we're apart, how long does it take for you to start missing me?
27. What do you think are the 3 most important things in a relationship?
28. What is your favorite gift you've ever received, and why was it your favorite?
29. What is one thing about your personality that you wish you could change?
30. What is the most important life lesson that you've learned so far?
31. Is there one moment in your life that you consider to be pivotal?
32. What is your deepest fear… other than snakes, spiders, etc?
33. What person in your life means the most to you, besides a family member?
34. What is your biggest weakness?
35. What single item is your most treasured possession, and why?
36. What are you most grateful for?
37. Do you think it's more important to live in the moment or plan for the future?
38. When do you feel the most loved? This is one of the MOST important conversations for couples to have!
39. What would you consider to be the biggest mistake you've ever made?
40. What is the biggest goal you have for yourself?

41. When do you feel the most at peace?
42. When is the last time you cried, other than at a movie or watching a tv show?
43. What is your favorite way to unwind at the end of a long day?
44. What is the kindest thing you have ever done for someone?
45. What is one of your favorite quotes?
46. What do you have to achieve in life for you to feel successful?
47. What stresses you out the most?
48. Who do you consider to be your best friend, and what character trait do you admire most about him or her?
49. What do you want to be your legacy?
50. What is your biggest pet peeve?
51. What accomplishment are you most proud of?
52. How would your best friend describe you?
53. Which of the Seven Deadly Sins are you most guilty of?
54. What are you most passionate about?
55. What are your two "non-negotiables" in a relationship?
56. What is the craziest thing you've ever done, that you would do again?
57. What is the worst advice you've ever been given?
58. What is the best advice you've ever been given?
59. What advice would you give to newlyweds?
60. What do you want to do after we retire?
61. What is one life lesson you hope to pass down to your kids?
62. What do you think our life will look like in 5 years?
63. What do you think our life will look like in 20 years?
64. If we ever get bored in our relationship, or things start to feel mundane, how do you think we should handle it?
65. What do you think we can do now to be better prepared for the future?
66. If I was not able to have kids, would that be a deal-breaker?

67. What is one tradition from your childhood that you want to pass down to your children?
68. What is the #1 thing on your bucket list?
69. How do you think we should celebrate our next anniversary?
70. What are some big decisions that you feel should always be made together?
71. What are your top 3 goals for your future?
72. What would your life look like if I were to die before you?
73. Do you think that couples who have lost "the spark" can still maintain a healthy relationship?
74. Do you think it's bad for a husband and wife to be best friends?
75. If you could go back and redo one moment in your life, what would it be and why?
76. If we had $1,000 extra each month, what would you want to do with it?
77. If you could meet any famous person, who would it be and why?
78. If we could go on ANY date, and the budget didn't matter, where would we go?
79. If we won $100,000 in the lottery, how would you want to spend it?
80. If you could live one day over and over again for the rest of your life, which day would it be?
81. What are the 3 items you would want if you were trapped on a deserted island (no boats/flair guns allowed!)?
82. If someone were to write a biography about you, what do you hope they would say?
83. If you could pick ANY fictional character to change places with, who would you choose and why?
84. We see a homeless man and his daughter holding up a sign… Do you stop and give him money or keep driving?
85. If I were to start making more money than you, would you feel like less of a man?
86. If we had to do one extracurricular activity together every day for a month, what would it be?

87. If a movie was made about our life, what actors would play us?
88. Money, power, love, or good looks... which would you choose?
89. If you were to lose your job tomorrow, what would you do?
90. If you could pick any job in the world to do, and money wasn't an issue, what would you choose?
91. If you could live one day over and over again for the rest of your life, which day would it be?
92. Of all of the restaurants that we've been to together, which is your favorite?
93. What is your biggest fear in life?
94. Were you ever sent to the principal's office as a kid? If so, why?
95. What is the one thing that I do that drives you the most nuts?
96. If I had to cook one meal for you for the rest of our lives, what would you want it to be?
97. What is the one thing you wish I did differently as a Mom/Dad?
98. What physical feature do you love most about me?
99. What physical feature of yours makes you the most self-conscious?
100. What do you love most about me?

with love!

Put a photo

or

Draw something

or

Write the conversation Starter

Date: .... Place: ....

....
....
....
....
....
....
....
....
....
....
....
....
....
....
....

Put a photo

or

Draw something

or

Write the conversation Starter

Date: .... Place:..........................

....
....
....
....
....
....
....
....
....
....
....
....
....
....

Put a photo
or
Draw something
or
Write the conversation Starter

Date: .... Place: ....

Put a photo

or

Draw something

or

Write the conversation Starter

Date: .... Place: ....

Put a photo
or
Draw something
or
Write the conversation Starter

Date: .... Place: ....

Put a photo

or

Draw something

or

Write the conversation Starter

Date: .... Place: ....

....
....
....
....
....
....
....
....
....
....
....
....
....
....

Put a photo

or

Draw something

or

Write the conversation Starter

Date: ……………… Place: ……………………

Put a photo

or

Draw something

or

Write the conversation Starter

Date: .... Place: ....

Put a photo

or

Draw something

or

Write the conversation Starter

Date: ……………… Place: ……………………

………
………
………
………
………
………
………
………
………
………
………
………
………
………

Put a photo
or
Draw something
or
Write the conversation Starter

Date: .... Place: ....

....
....
....
....
....
....
....
....
....
....
....
....
....
....
....

Put a photo
or
Draw something
or
Write the conversation Starter

Date: .... Place: ....

Put a photo

or

Draw something

or

Write the conversation Starter

Date: .... Place:..........................

....
....
....
....
....
....
....
....
....
....
....
....
....
....
....

Put a photo

or

Draw something

or

Write the conversation Starter

Date: .... Place: ....

....
....
....
....
....
....
....
....
....
....
....
....
....
....
....

Put a photo

or

Draw something

or

Write the conversation Starter

Date: .... Place:..........................

Put a photo

or

Draw something

or

Write the conversation Starter

Date: .... Place:...........................

Put a photo
or
Draw something
or
Write the conversation Starter

Date: .... Place: ....

Put a photo

or

Draw something

or

Write the conversation Starter

Date: .... Place: ....

....
....
....
....
....
....
....
....
....
....
....
....
....
....

Put a photo

or

Draw something

or

Write the conversation Starter

Date: .... Place: ....

....
....
....
....
....
....
....
....
....
....
....
....
....
....

Put a photo

or

Draw something

or

Write the conversation Starter

Date: .... Place:..........................

Put a photo

or

Draw something

or

Write the conversation Starter

Date: .... Place: ....

Put a photo

or

Draw something

or

Write the conversation Starter

Date: ……………… Place: ……………………………

……………………………………………………………………………………
……………………………………………………………………………………
……………………………………………………………………………………
……………………………………………………………………………………
……………………………………………………………………………………
……………………………………………………………………………………
……………………………………………………………………………………
……………………………………………………………………………………
……………………………………………………………………………………
……………………………………………………………………………………
……………………………………………………………………………………
……………………………………………………………………………………
……………………………………………………………………………………
……………………………………………………………………………………
……………………………………………………………………………………

Put a photo

or

Draw something

or

Write the conversation Starter

Date: .... Place: ....

....
....
....
....
....
....
....
....
....
....
....
....
....
....
....

Put a photo

or

Draw something

or

Write the conversation Starter

Date: ……………… Place:………………………

Put a photo

or

Draw something

or

Write the conversation Starter

Date: .... Place:...........................

....
....
....
....
....
....
....
....
....
....
....
....
....
....

Put a photo

or

Draw something

or

Write the conversation Starter

Date: .... Place: ....

Put a photo

or

Draw something

or

Write the conversation Starter

Date: .... Place: ....

Put a photo

or

Draw something

or

Write the conversation Starter

Date: .... Place:...........................

....

....

....

....

....

....

....

....

....

....

....

....

....

....

Put a photo

or

Draw something

or

Write the conversation Starter

Date: .... Place: ....

Put a photo

or

Draw something

or

Write the conversation Starter

Date: .... Place: ....

....
....
....
....
....
....
....
....
....
....
....
....
....
....
....

Put a photo
or
Draw something
or
Write the conversation Starter

Date: .... Place: ....

....
....
....
....
....
....
....
....
....
....
....
....
....
....
....
....

Put a photo

or

Draw something

or

Write the conversation Starter

Date: .... Place:...........................

....

....

....

....

....

....

....

....

....

....

....

....

....

....

Put a photo

or

Draw something

or

Write the conversation Starter

Date: ……………… Place: ………………………

Put a photo

or

Draw something

or

Write the conversation Starter

Date: .... Place: ....

Put a photo

or

Draw something

or

Write the conversation Starter

Date: .... Place: ....

....

....

....

....

....

....

....

....

....

....

....

....

....

....

Put a photo

or

Draw something

or

Write the conversation Starter

Date: .... Place:..........................

....
....
....
....
....
....
....
....
....
....
....
....
....
....
....

Put a photo

or

Draw something

or

Write the conversation Starter

Date: .... Place:...........................

Put a photo

or

Draw something

or

Write the conversation Starter

Date: .... Place:........................

Put a photo

or

Draw something

or

Write the conversation Starter

Date: .... Place: ....

....
....
....
....
....
....
....
....
....
....
....
....
....
....

Put a photo

or

Draw something

or

Write the conversation Starter

Date: ……………… Place: ……………………

Put a photo

or

Draw something

or

Write the conversation Starter

Date: .... Place: ....

....
....
....
....
....
....
....
....
....
....
....
....
....
....
....

Put a photo

or

Draw something

or

Write the conversation Starter

Date: .... Place: ....

....

....

....

....

....

....

....

....

....

....

....

....

....

....

Put a photo

or

Draw something

or

Write the conversation Starter

Date: .... Place: ....

Put a photo

or

Draw something

or

Write the conversation Starter

Date: .... Place:........................

Put a photo

or

Draw something

or

Write the conversation Starter

Date: .... Place: ....

Put a photo

or

Draw something

or

Write the conversation Starter

Date: .... Place: ....

....

....

....

....

....

....

....

....

....

....

....

....

....

....

Put a photo

or

Draw something

or

Write the conversation Starter

Date: .... Place: ....

Put a photo

or

Draw something

or

Write the conversation Starter

Date: .... Place: ....

Thanks for everything

Thank you so much for trying our Adventure Book for Couples!
We'd love to hear from you!

If you've found this to be a good book please,
support us and leave a review.

If you have any suggestions or issues with this journal, or if
you want to test some of our latest books
please email us.

Send email to:
pickme.readme@gmail.com

Copyrights @ 2022
All rights reserved

You may not reproduce, duplicate, or send the contents of this book without direct written permission from the author. You cannot hereby despite any circumstance blame the publisher or hold him or her the legal responsibility for any reparation, compensation or monetary forfeiture owing to the information included herein, either in a direct or indirect way.

Legal Notice: This book has copyright protection. You can use the book for personal purpose. You should not sell, use, alter, distribute, quote, take excerpts or paraphrase in part of whole the material contained in this book without obtaining the permission of the author first.

Disclaimer Notice: You must take note that the information in this document is for casual reading and entertainment purpose only. We have made every attempt to provide accurate, up to date and reliable information. We do not express or imply guarantees of any kind. The person who read admit that the writer is not occupied in giving legal, financial, medical, or other advice. We put this book content by sourcing various places.

Please consult a licensed professional before you try any techniques shown in this book.By going through this document, the book lover comes to an agreement that under no situation is the author accountable for any forfeiture, direct or indirect, which they may incur because of the use of material contained in this document, including, but not limited to, - errors, omissions, or inaccuracies.